Table of Contents

System Requirements 1

Installation Instructions. 1

CONTACCT Planner. 2

Case - Fred and Ned's Sandwhich Sled. 9

Module I. 15

Module II. 20

Module III. 24

Module IV. 31

Module V. 39

Module VI. 49

Appendix I

T-Account documents Module V.. 57

CONTACCT

II

Consultant for Teaching Accounting

Version 3

by D.V. Rama
and K. Raghunandan

SOUTH-WESTERN College Publishing

An International Thomson Publishing Company

ISBN 0-538-87585-2

CONTACCT II

Constultant for Teaching Accounting

Hello - Welcome to CONTACCT! CONTACCT is a computer-assisted instruction software package. CONTACCT consists of tutorials, practice assignments and graded assignments to help you learn the accounting cycle. The following pages describe the functions and features of CONTACCT, and some information that will help you to start and use CONTACCT.

SYSTEM REQUIREMENTS

The minimum system requirements to run CONTACCT are:

* A personal computer with an 80486 processor or higher
* Microsoft Windows version 3.1, Windows 95, Windows NT 3.5 or higher
* DOS 3.1 or higher
* 8 MB of RAM (12 MB recommended)
* One 1.4 MB (3.5") disk drive
* A hard disk with 10 MB of free disk space
* A graphics adapter card (VGA, Super VGA or other Windows-compatible card) capable of displaying at least 256 colors at 640x 480 resolution
* A mouse or other Windows-compatible pointing device

INSTALLATION INSTRUCTIONS

To install CONTACCT II to your hard drive, perform the following steps:

1. Start Windows 3.1, Windows 95 or higher, or Windows NT
2. Insert Disk 1 in Drive A or B
3. From the File Menu or the Start Taskbar choose RUN
4. TYPE A:\ (or B:\) SETUP and press ENTER

The install program will copy files to your hard drive. It will then prompt you for the program group that will contain the CONTACCT icon. The default name is CONTACCT. After the program group and icon are created, installation is complete

CONTACCT PLANNER

This section summarizes the topics covered by CONTACCT and provides information for planning your work on CONTACCT. CONTACCT consists of six modules, plus a module that contains comprehensive problems. Each module,with the exception of the comprehensive problems module, covers two or more topics. The module contains tutorials, practice problems and graded problems on each topic. Tutorials provide detailed explanations of concepts and present worked examples to help you complete assignments. Review questions are presented during the tutorial to reinforce concepts.

After completing a tutorial, you can complete practice problems to ensure that you have understood the material covered in the tutorial. CONTACCT provides help in different ways while you are working on practice problems. While solving a practice problem you can

- refer to the tutorial
- refer to a demonstration problem
- ask the consultant for detailed directions on solving the problem
- look up key terms in a glossary

Finally, you can complete the graded problems. There is a set of multiple choice questions on each topic. Matching problems require you to match descriptions of concepts with appropriate terms from a list of concepts. In addition, there are several problems similar to the worked examples and practice problems.

You may use CONTACCT in different ways. One possible plan for working on CONTACCT is shown on this page.

Possible Schedule for Using CONTACCT

Session Number	Module	Topic
1	1	Transaction analysis
2		Transaction analysis; Accounting equation
3		Transaction analysis; Accounting equation
4		Journalizing and posting transactions
5		Journalizing and posting transactions
6		Financial statements
7		Revenue and expense recognition
8,9,10		Comprehensive problems
11		Adjusting entries
12		Adjusting entries
13		Closing entries
14,15		Comprehensive problems

STARTING CONTACCT

NOTE: MAKE SURE THAT CONTACCT HAS BEEN INSTALLED BEFORE FOLLOWING THESE INSTRUCTIONS.

The software is installed with an icon named CONTACCT. To start CONTACCT, start Windows, insert the Disk 4 of 4 in the A or B drive (this is now your data disk), open the CONTACCT Program Group and double click on the **CONTACCT** Icon.

After the introductory screens, the main menu screen shown below will be displayed. If you are using the system for the first time, the system will ask you for your name before allowing you to select a module. Once you have entered your name, you will not be allowed to change it. Your name will appear on all printouts.

Click on a module to select it

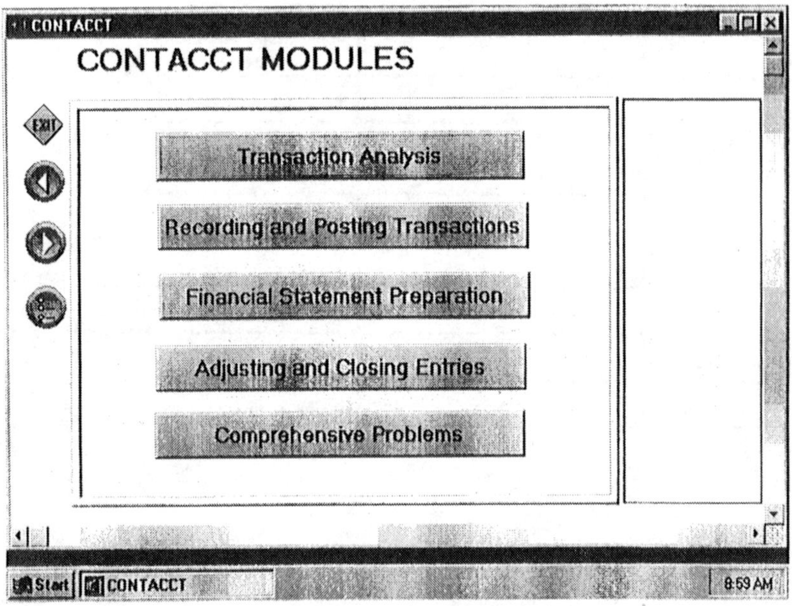

ENDING A SESSION

To exit the program, click on the **EXIT** button on the main menu screen. Click on the **PRINT** button to print a record of your work. The system prints a list of all assignments and tutorials completed with your name and the current date. Note that the system puts check marks against an assignment (tutorial) only if you have completed that assignment (tutorial).

To exit from CONTACCT when you are working on an assignment or tutorial, click on the **Menu** button to return to the main menu screen. Exit the program from the main menu screen as explained above.

USAGE NOTES

A typical screen in CONTACCT is shown below:

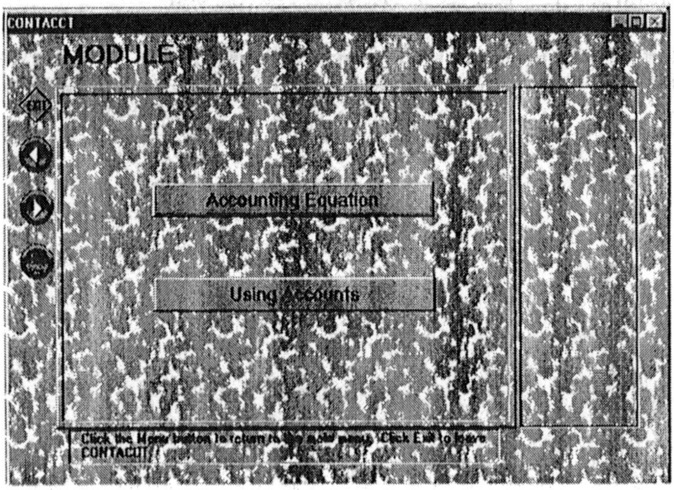

Every screen in CONTACCT has a similar organization. The following are typical components found on every screen:

Title	The title area at the top, left-hand corner describes the contents of the current screen.
Instructions	The bottom of the screen gives directions for working on the assignment or tutorial.
Buttons	Buttons are important tools for moving around in CONTACCT. Some commonly used buttons are listed on the next page.

List of Frequently Used Buttons

Right arrow	After completing the activities required on the current screen, click the Right Arrow to proceed with the assignment or tutorial. If there are no instructions at the bottom of a CONTACCT screen, read the information on the current screen and press the Right Arrow.
Left Arrow	Use the Left Arrow button to go to the previous screen. For example, you could move back in the tutorial to review some concept which was explained previously.
Menu	If you are working on an assignment or tutorial, click on the button to return to the main menu screen.
Next Transaction	Use the NEXT TRANSACTION button to to to the next transaction in assignments or tutorials
Previous Transaction	Use the PREVIOUS TRANSACTION button to go to the previous transaction in assignments or tutorials.
Glossary	Click on the GLOSSARY button to look up short explanations of important concepts.
Solution	This button is available only in Practice Problems. If you click on the SOLUTION button the system will display the solution and explanation to the current problem.
Tutorial	This button is available only in assignments. If you click on the TUTORIAL button, the system will present a tutorial related to the current assignment.
Assignment	This button is available only in tutorials. If you switched to a tutorial from an assignment, click on the ASSIGNMENT button to return to the assignment.

Fred and Ned's Sandwich Sled

This case consists of seven parts. Each part of the case includes assignments and tutorials to be completed on CONTACCT, as well as manual exercises. This section describes the exercises and CONTACCT assignments for Fred and Ned's Sandwich Shop.

List of CONTACCT assignments

Part	Module	Topic	Practice Problem
I	1	Using Accounts	2
II	2	Owners' Equity Transactions	2
III	3	Financial Statements	2
IV	3	Revenue and Expense Recognition	2
V	4	Accruals Deferrals	2
VI	4	Closing entries	1

Fred and Ned's Sandwich Sled

The following pages describe the different parts of the case. The description is organized into six parts corresponding to the six CONTACCT assignments related to the case. The name of the assignment corresponding to each section is listed in the section heading. Each part consists of assignments to be completed on CONTACCT as well as discussion questions/exercises. The tasks to be completed on CONTACCT are marked with *.

The following narrative applies to parts I, II and III.

Fred and his brother have headed Northwest from Boston during the spring of 1998 hoping to make their fortune in a booming mining village in Alaska. They had owned a restaurant in Boston and planned to establish a food service business in a remote village.

When they arrived in the small town they located a boarding house called Nellie's Place. The owner, Nellie, agreed to sell them sandwiches for $1.50 each and large jugs of coffee for $2.00 (each jug holds approximately 10 cups of coffee). They planned to use sleds pulled by dogs to transport the food to remote mining locations. They obtained permission from the mine owner to park one sled loaded with sandwiches and coffee at the entrance to the Golden Nugget Mine and another sled at the entrance to the King Solomon Mine. They decided to charge the miners $2.00 for each sandwich and $0.50 for each cup of coffee. They began operations on July 1, 1998. Fred and Ned's activities for July 1998 are listed below:

July 1	Fred and Ned invested $5,000 in "Fred and Ned's Sandwich Sled".
July 2	The business purchased 1,250 lbs of dog food for $125.
July 3	Fred and Ned rented a house for $1,800 per year for personal use.
July 3	The business rented sleds, harnesses and dogs for $200 per month. The rent for July will be paid at the end of July.
July 5	The business purchased sandwiches for $1,500 and coffee for $850. They paid $1,000 to Nellie for these items.
July 31	During the month Fred and Ned collected $4,200 from miners for the sandwiches and coffee. Occasionally, when a miner is short of funds IOUs are accepted instead of payment. At the end of July, there are $400 of IOU slips.
July 31	The cost of goods sold for the month was $2,350, assuming that any sandwiches not sold during a week are thrown away.
July 31	Dog food worth $100 was used during the month.
July 31	Fred and Ned's business paid the rent of $200 for the dogs and sleds.
July 31	Fred and Ned's business paid $50 to a local farmer who kept the dogs at his farm during the nights and weekends.

Part I

*1. Complete the tutorials in module 1 of CONTACCT.

2. Prepare answers to the following questions:

a. Based on the description in the previous page, develop a list of decisions that Fred and Ned may need to make in the operation of their business.
b. Discuss what types of information Fred and Ned could use to improve their decision-making.
c. Study the activities listed on the previous page and discuss which of these activities should be recorded in the accounting system of Fred and Ned.

*3. Start CONTACCT and select *Module 1* (Transaction Analysis). CONTACCT will display a list of topics in this module. Select the *topic* "Using Accounts". A list of tasks for this module will now be displayed. Select *practice problem* 2. This assignment requires you to analyze the transactions for Fred and Ned's Sandwich Sled and show that the accounting equation remains in balance after every transaction. The system will check your solution. If the answer is incorrect, the system shows the correct solution with an explanation. You can also refer to a tutorial or glossary of related terms as you are working on the assignment.

4. Discuss why the accounting equation must remain in balance after every transaction.

Part II

*1. Complete the tutorials in module 2 of CONTACCT.

2. Prepare answers to the following questions:
a) Discuss the meaning of the following terms: 1) journal 2) general ledger and 3) chart of accounts.
b) Based on the description of Fred and Ned's Sandwich Sled and the list of transactions in July 1998, prepare a chart (list) of accounts for Fred and Ned's accounting system.
c) Classify each of the above accounts into an asset, liability, owners' equity, revenue or expense accounts.
d) Describe the debit/credit rules for an asset, liability and owners' equity accounts.

*3. Start CONTACCT and select *Module 2* (Recording and Posting Transactions). CONTACCT will display a list of topics in this module. Select the *topic* "Owners' Equity Transactions". A list of tasks for this module will now be displayed. Select *practice problem* 2. This assignment requires you to prepare journal entries for Fred and Ned's Sandwich Sled for July 1998. The system will check your solution. If the answer is incorrect, the system shows the correct solution with an explanation.

You can also refer to a tutorial or glossary of related terms as you are working on the assignment.

Part III

Note: **Read parts 3 and 4 before starting part 3 on CONTACCT.**

*1. Complete the tutorial on financial statements in module 3 of CONTACCT.

2. Prepare answers to the following questions:

a) Describe the purpose and content of the following statements:
1) Income Statement
2) Statement of Retained Earnings
3) Balance Sheet

b) What is the normal balance (debit or credit) in the following types of accounts:
1) Capital Stock
2) Accounts Payable
3) Supplies
4) Cost of Goods Sold
5) Dividends

*3 **(Note: Read question 4 and 5 before starting this assignment. These questions require you to note down some of the information from the financial statements displayed by CONTACCT.)**
Start CONTACCT and select *Module 3* (Financial Statement Preparation). CONTACCT will display a list of topics in this module. Select the *topic* "Financial Statements". A list of tasks for this module will now be displayed. Select *practice problem* 2. This assignment requires you to specify which accounts in Fred and Ned's accounting system will appear on the income statement and the balance sheet. You will also be asked to complete a statement of Retained Earnings for Fred and Ned's Sandwich Sled.

4. What is the balance shown in the Retained Earnings Account in the trial balance displayed by the system? What is the balance shown in the Retained Earnings Account in the balance sheet? Why are these numbers different?

5. Discuss how the ending balance in Retained Earnings is computed.

Fred and Ned's Sandwich Sled

The following description applies to parts IV and V.

Fred and Ned's business has met with incredible success in their first month of operations. Hence they have decided to expand their business. They obtain financing from the bank to purchase the assets needed to start a restaurant. They do not want to give up the sandwich sleds because they feel that selling food at the mine will keep them in touch with the miners and attract more business to the restaurant on the weekends. That means they will need to hire some employees to operate either the sleds or the restaurant. Nellie agrees to work as an on-site manager at the saloon when Fred and Ned are at the mines. They also hire a bartender, a cook and two people to wait tables and clean up.

The transactions for August are shown below:

Aug 1	Fred and Ned's business borrowed $12,000 from the bank in exchange for a 10%, two year note payable.
Aug 1	A building was rented for $800 per month. Three months rent was paid in advance.
Aug 2	Dog food supplies were purchased for $120.
Aug 2	Equipment was purchased for $7,200. The equipment consists of furniture and fixtures, stove, refrigerator, beer tap and cash register.
Aug 5	Inventory was purchased for $5,400. $2,500 was paid in cash.
Aug 10	The miners paid $400 for the sandwiches and coffee sold to them in July.
Aug 12	$1,350 was paid to Nellie for inventory purchased in July.
Aug 31	The business earned $9,000. $6,100 was collected in cash.
Aug 31	The cost of the goods sold was $5,400.
Aug 31	Dog food supplies worth $125 were consumed.
Aug 31	Rent of $250 was paid for August. (This amount includes the rent on the sleds, harnesses and dogs, and the rent paid to the farmer.)
Aug 31	Salaries of $900 were paid to employees.

Part IV

*1. Complete the tutorial on revenue and expense recognition in module 3 of CONTACCT.

*2. Start CONTACCT and select *Module 3* (Financial Statement Preparation). CONTACCT will display a list of topics in this module. Select the *topic* "Revenue and Expense Recognition". A list of tasks for this module will now be displayed. Select *practice problem* 2. This assignment requires you to analyze transactions for August 1998 and specify whether these transactions involve the recognition of revenues or expenses. The system will check your solution. If the answer is incorrect, the system shows the correct solution with an explanation. You can also refer to a tutorial or glossary of related terms as you are working on the assignment.

3. Prepare answers to the following questions:

a) Write brief explanations of the following terms:

1) Matching principle

2) Accrual versus cash basis

3) Periodicity

b) Fred and Ned's Sandwich Sled purchased several resources including 1)supplies 2) inventory and 3) equipment. Based on the principles discussed in tutorial 6, discuss when the cost of these resources are recognized as expenses by Fred and Ned's business.

Part V

*1. Complete tutorials on accruals and deferrals in module 4 of CONTACCT.

*2 Start CONTACCT and select *Module 4* (Adjusting and Closing Entries). CONTACCT will display a list of topics in this module. Select the *topic* "Accruals". A list of tasks for this module will now be displayed. Select *practice problem* 2. This assignment requires you to record the adjustments listed below for August 1998.

*3 Start CONTACCT and select *Module 4* (Adjusting and Closing Entries). CONTACCT will display a list of topics in this module. Select the *topic* "Deferrals". A list of tasks for this module will now be displayed. Select *practice problem* 2. This assignment requires you to record the adjustments listed below for August 1998.

4. Prepare answers to the following questions:

a. Discuss the terms "accrued expenses" and "deferred expenses".

b. If Fred and Ned do not make the adjusting entry for depreciation, what will be the impact on the net income and total assets for August 1998? Discuss whether net income and assets will be overstated or understated.

5. Discuss the following statements based on the transactions occurring in August 1998:

a. "The net income for August 1998 includes the $400 collected from customers on August 10."

b. "The $100 owed to the dishwasher for services provided in August should be included in computing net income for August."

c. "The payment to Nellie on August 12 represents an expense for August and must be included in the computation of net income for August."

Part VI

*1. Complete the tutorial on closing entries in module 4 of CONTACCT.

*2. Start CONTACCT and select *Module 4* (Adjusting and Closing Entries). CONTACCT

will display a list of topics in this module. Select the *topic* "Closing Entries". A list of tasks for this module will now be displayed. Select *practice problem* 1.
This assignment requires you to record the closing entries listed below for July 1998.

Jul. 31	Close the revenue accounts.
Jul. 31	Close the expense accounts
Jul. 31	Close the Income Summary account.

You can look up the required account balances as you are working on CONTACCT.

Part VII
Internal Control

As discussed in the previous parts, Fred and Ned started a restaurant in addition to their sandwich sled operations in August 1998. Nellie agreed to work as an on-site manager at the saloon when Fred and Ned are at the mines. They also hired a bartender, a cook and two people to wait tables and clean up.

Fred was concerned about having the restaurant open when neither he nor Ned can be there to keep an eye on things. He was also concerned about keeping track of the payroll information for all of the new employees. Ned suggested the following procedures regarding payroll.

Each employee will keep track of their own payroll hours. At the end of each week, a listing of these hours will be submitted to Fred for approval. Fred will compute the amount each employee has earned and give this information to Nellie. Nellie will prepare the payroll checks for Fred's signature and maintain a record of the amounts paid to each employee. After Fred signs the checks, he will give them back to Nellie for distribution to the employees.

1. Discuss the internal control weaknesses in the above payroll procedure.
2. Suggest improvements to the payroll procedure described in the above narrative.

CHAPTER 3
TUTORIALS

This chapter shows selected screens from all the tutorials. The numbers of the screen in the tutorial is also listed (for example, *2 of 16)*. These screens contain explanations of important concepts covered in each tutorial.

MODULE I

TRANSACTION ANALYSIS

I. ACCOUNTING EQUATION

Tutorial - Selected Screens

1 of 16
After completing this tutorial you should be able to use the accounting equation in analyzing business transactions.

2 of 16
Overview
Accounting is a system used for recording, summarizing and communicating economic information. Decision-makers use accounting information to make decisions about the use of scarce economic resources such as money and labor.

Several typical activities are performed by all business organizations. First, businesses acquire money from investors (owners) or creditors (lenders). Financial resources are used to buy other resources such as land, equipment and supplies. These resources are used in producing and selling goods or services. The sale of goods and services produces additional monetary resources. The accounting system analyzes, records, classifies and stores information about such business activities.

3 of 16
Users of accounting information
A range of people use accounting information to make decisions. Some examples are given below:

Investors provide money to businesses and expect to share in its earnings. Investors use accounting information to evaluate risk and return on investments. They need accounting information to decide whether to maintain, increase or decrease the investment in a business.

4 of 16
Users of accounting information
Creditors loan money to organizations for a specific period and a specific rate of return. Potential creditors use accounting information for making loan decisions.

Managers need accounting information for decision-making. These decisions relate to the type and amount of resources to be purchased, timing of purchases, etc. Other users of accounting information include employees, customers and suppliers.

5 of 16

Assets & Liabilities

Assets are economic resources that are owned or controlled by an entity for future benefits. Examples of assets include cash, inventory (goods for resale), equipment, land and buildings.

Liabilities are economic obligations of an organization to pay cash or transfer other resources. For example, businesses often borrow from banks or other lending institutions. These amounts must be paid to the creditors in the future. Thus a liability is recorded for the amounts owed to creditors.

8 of 16

Owners' Equity

Investors provide money or other resources to a business. Businesses obtain additional resources by selling goods and services at a profit. These profits could be distributed to owners or reinvested in the business.

Owners' equity includes the amounts originally invested and any profits reinvested in the business.

9 of 16

Transactions Increasing Owners' Equity

When an owner invests money in a business, owners' equity increases. The increase in equity is matched by an increase in assets(cash).

Revenue is the price of goods sold or services sold by a business during a given period. Revenues increase the owners' equity in the business. If the business sells goods/services and collects cash, the increase in owners' equity matches the increase in cash.

10 of 16

Transactions Decreasing Owners' Equity

Expenses represent the cost of resources used in producing, selling or delivering goods and services. Examples of expenses include utilities, rent and salaries.

Expenses cause a decrease in owners' equity. If the business pays for the resources, then the decrease in owners' equity is matched by a decrease in cash.

Owners' equity also decreases when an owner withdraws money from a business or when cash is distributed to the owners.

11 of 16

The accounting equation shown below represents the relationship between an organization's assets, liabilities and owners' equity:

Assets = Liabilities +Owners' Equity

Organizations need various resources for producing and selling goods/services. These are acquired with the financial resources provided by creditors (liabilities) or investors (owners' equity). This equation must remain in balance after every transaction. Thus each transaction increases or decreases both sides of the equation by equal amounts.

16 of 16
Summary
Assets are resources. These are acquired with the financial resources provided by creditors (liabilities) or owners (owners' equity).

The accounting equation states that the sum of the liabilities and owners' equity equals total assets.

The accounting equation must remain in balance after every transaction. Thus each transaction increases or decreases both sides of the equation by equal amounts.

II. USING ACCOUNTS

Tutorial - Selected Screens

1 of 16
Learning Objectives
After completing this tutorial you should be able to:

Describe the different types of accounts used for recording information about transactions.
Identify the accounts affected by different transactions.

2 of 16
Account
An account is the basic unit for recording data in the accounting system. An account is a record of increases and decreases in the dollar amount associated with each asset, liability and owners' equity item. For example, every cash receipt or payment is recorded as a change to the Cash account. Five types of accounts are used in the accounting system.

Assets
Liabilities
Owners' Equity
Revenues
Expenses

3 of 16
Assets
Assets are economic resources that are owned or controlled by an entity for future benefits.

Examples of asset accounts include Cash, Accounts Receivable, Inventory, Supplies, Equipment, Land and Buildings.

Accounts Receivable are amounts owed by customers on credit sales. When an organization sells goods/services on credit, Accounts Receivable is increased. Subsequently, when payments are made by customers, Accounts Receivable is decreased.

4 of 16
Assets
Merchandise for sale is called inventory. When such merchandise is purchased or manufactured it

is recorded as an asset (Inventory). The inventory account decreases when the goods are sold.

Supplies include office supplies (paper, diskettes, etc.), cleaning supplies, etc. When supplies are purchased, they are recorded as an asset called Supplies. The Supplies account decreases as the supplies are used.

Fixed assets or plant assets provide long-term benefits to the business. Examples of fixed assets include land, buildings and equipment.

5 of 16

Liabilities

Liabilities are economic obligations of an organization to pay cash or transfer other resources. Liabilities primarily include amounts owed by an organization to its creditors. Examples of liabilities include Accounts Payable and Notes Payable.

Accounts Payable represents amounts owed to suppliers for credit purchases. Accounts Payable increases when goods/services are purchased on credit. Accounts Payable decreases when payment is made to suppliers for prior credit purchases.

6 of 16

Liabilities

Notes Payable represents amounts borrowed from banks and other lending institutions. A notes payable is a formal written promise to pay the amount borrowed as well as interest at a definite time. Notes Payable increases when money is borrowed from creditors and decreases when creditors are paid back.

9 of 16

Owners' equity

Recall that owners' equity includes the amounts invested by owners in a business as well as reinvested profits.

Revenue is the price of goods sold or services sold by a business during a given period. Revenues increase the owners' equity in the business. If the business sells goods/services and collects cash, the increase in owners' equity matches the increase in cash.

When goods/services are sold on credit, owners' equity is increased. Accounts Receivable is also increased by an equal amount.

10 of 16

Expenses

Expenses represent the cost of resources used in producing, selling or delivering goods and services. Examples of expenses include rent expense, utilities expense, salaries expense, supplies expense and cost of goods sold.

Salaries Expense is the amount earned by employees for services performed during the period.

Supplies Expense is the cost of supplies used during a period. When supplies are used, supplies expense is recorded and the asset supplies is decreased by the same amount.

11 of 16

Expenses

Cost of Goods Sold is the cost of the merchandise sold to customers. Recall that when merchandise for sale is purchased it is recorded as an asset (inventory). When the goods are sold, their cost is recorded as an expense and the inventory account is decreased by an equal amount.

16 of 16

Summary

An account is a record of increases and decreases in the dollar amount associated with a specific resource or activity. An account is the basic unit for recording data in the accounting system.

Transactions are recorded in an accounting system using five types of accounts:

Assets (cash, accounts receivable, supplies etc.)
Liabilities (notes payable, accounts payable)
Owners' equity
Revenues
Expenses (cost of goods sold, supplies expense, rent expense, utilities expense, salaries expense)

MODULE II
RECORDING AND POSTING TRANSACTIONS

I. RECORDING TRANSACTIONS

Tutorial - Selected Screens

1 of 19
Learning Objectives
After completing this tutorial you should be able to:

Record the transactions in a journal.
Post the transactions to the general ledger.

2 of 19
Overview
Previous tutorials described the accounts used for recording transactions. These tutorials also discussed the analysis of transactions to determine their effect on accounts. After analyzing the effect of transactions on asset, liability and owners' equity accounts, the information about these transactions is recorded in a set of accounting books. This tutorial describes double-entry bookkeeping, a systematic method for recording transactions in the accounting system.

3 of 19
Double-Entry Bookkeeping
The term double-entry comes from the requirement that each transaction be recorded in at least two accounts. Recall the accounting equation:

ASSETS = LIABILITIES + OWNERS' EQUITY

This equation must remain in balance at all times. Therefore, if one element in the equation changes, some other elements must also change to maintain the balance. Thus at least two accounts will be affected by every transaction.

4 of 19
General Ledger
The general ledger is used to record the impact of transactions on accounts. Two columns are used to record the increases and decreases to an account respectively. These columns form a "T" .as shown in the above figure. Thus the general ledger is also referred to as T-accounts. One T-account is used for each account in the accounting books. The column on the left side of the T-account is called the debit side. The column on the right side is called the credit side.

5 of 19
Assets and liabilities
The side used for recording increases is based on the accounting equation shown below:

Assets are on the left side of the above equation. As shown below increases in assets are recorded in the column on the left (the debit) side.

6 of 19

Liabilities and Owners' Equity

Liabilities and owners' equity appear on the right side of the accounting equation. Hence, increases in liabilities and owners' equity are recorded on the right (the credit) side. For example, Notes Payable is credited for increases and debited for decreases.

7 of 19

Revenues and Expenses

Owners' equity is increased when the business earns revenue. Owners' equity is credited for increases. Thus revenues are recorded by crediting the appropriate revenue accounts.

Owners' equity is decreased when the business incurs an expense. Owners' equity is debited for decreases. Thus expenses are recorded by debiting the appropriate expense accounts.

10 of 19

General Journal

A journal is a book for recording transactions in the order in which they occur. Transactions are recorded in the journal after being analyzed to determine which accounts are affected, the amount of the effect, and whether the transaction increases or decreases these accounts. As shown below, the journal identifies the date of the transaction, the accounts affected by the transaction and the amounts. After the transaction is recorded in the journal, it is posted to T-accounts (general ledger).

11 of 19

General Ledger

After the transaction is recorded in the journal, it is posted to T-accounts (general ledger). The transaction shown on the previous page is posted to two T-accounts shown below. Note that both the general journal and the general ledger contain information about accounts and the amount by which these accounts are debited or credited. The difference is in the organization of information. The information is organized by account in the general ledger. Thus accountants use the general ledger to calculate balances in different accounts.

19 of 19

Summary

The traditional approach used to process transactions is known as double-entry bookkeeping since each transaction must be recorded in at least two accounts.

A journal is a book for recording transactions in the order in which they occur.

The general ledger is used to systematically record increases and decreases in account balances resulting from different transactions.

Two columns are used to record the increases and decreases to an account respectively. The column on the left side of the account is called the debit side and the right side is called the credit side.

II. OWNERS' EQUITY TRANSACTIONS

Tutorial - Selected Screens

1 of 16
Learning Objectives
After completing this tutorial you should be able to:

Describe the different types of business organizations.
Record information about owner investments and withdrawals/dividends.

2 of 16
Forms of Business Organizations
A business organization may be organized as a sole proprietorship, partnership or a corporation.

A sole proprietorship is a business owned by one person. Usually the owner is actively involved in its operations. The owner manages the day-to-day activities of the business and realizes the profits (or losses) from the business. From an accounting standpoint, the owner and the business are distinct entities. The owner's resources or personal financial activities must not be included in the accounting records of the business. However, legally the sole proprietor and his business are not separate entities. Thus the proprietor is personally liable for the debts of the business.

3 of 16
Journal Entry- Owner Investments
This screen shows how owner investments in sole-proprietorships are recorded in the accounting system. When the owner makes an investment, the increase in money is recorded as a debit to the Cash account. The investment also increases the owner's equity in the business. For sole-proprietorship, the owner's equity account is called the Owner's Capital account. Investments are recorded by crediting the Owner's Capital account.

4 of 16
Journal Entry - Owner Withdrawal
This screen shows how owner withdrawals in sole-proprietorships are recorded in the accounting system. When the owner withdraws money invested in the business, the decrease in money is recorded as a credit to the Cash account. Withdrawals also decrease the owner's equity in the business. For proprietorships, this decrease in owner's equity is recorded in a Drawings account. The Owner's Drawings account is debited since the owner's equity is decreased by this transaction.

9 of 16
Corporations
A corporation is recognized under the law as a distinct entity from the owners. The owners of the corporation are not personally liable for the debts of the business. The owners of the corporation have limited liability since they cannot lose any more than the amounts invested in the business.

Ownership of the corporation is divided into shares of capital stock and the owners are called stockholders. Owners can sell all or part of their shares to other investors. Managers of a corporation manage the day-to-day operations of the business. Managers may or may not be stockholders. Thus there is a separation of ownership and management of corporations.

10 of 16

Journal Entry - Owner Investments

The corporation has issued stock. This transaction involves the receipt of money from owners. The increase in money is recorded as a debit to the Cash account. This investment also increases the owners' equity in the business. For a corporation, owner investments are recorded by crediting the Capital Stock account.

11 of 16

Journal Entry - Dividends

The corporation has issued dividends. This transaction involves the payment of money to owners. The decrease in money is recorded as a credit to the Cash account. The dividend also decreases the owners' equity in the business. The reduction in owners' equity is recorded as a debit to the Dividends account. The Dividends account is used for recording dividends declared during a period. At the end of the period this amount is transferred to the Retained Earnings account.

16 of 16

Summary

A corporation is recognized under the law as a distinct entity from the owners. The owners of the corporation are not personally liable for the debts of the business. A sole-proprietorship is not recognized as a separate legal entity. Both sole-proprietorships and corporations are considered as distinct entities from an accounting standpoint.

Sole-proprietorships use the Capital account to record investments. Withdrawals by owners are recorded in the Drawings account.

Corporations use the Capital Stock account to record investments. The Retained Earnings account is used to record reinvested profits.

MODULE III

I. FINANCIAL STATEMENTS

Tutorial - Selected Screens

1 of 22
Learning Objectives
After completing this tutorial you should be able to:

Prepare a trial balance.
Prepare an income statement.
Prepare a balance sheet.

2 of 22
Overview
The accounting cycle includes all the steps from the occurrence of various transactions to the preparation of the financial statements. Previous tutorials described the following two steps:

- Analyze and record transactions in journal.
- Post transactions to ledger.

This tutorial describes two steps which are completed after posting transactions to the ledger:
- Prepare trial balance.
- Prepare financial statements.

3 of 22
Account balance - Asset Accounts
Assets are increased by debits. Therefore, the normal balance in asset accounts is a debit balance. Cash is debited when cash is received. Cash is credited when cash is paid. A credit balance would imply that the organization has a negative amount of Cash. Thus usually we would expect a debit balance in the Cash account. In the example shown below the Cash account has been debited by $10,500 for receipts and credited by $2,500 for payments resulting in a debit balance of $8,000.

4 of 22
Accounts Balances - Liability Accounts
Liabilities are increased by credits. When amounts owed to creditors or suppliers increase, a liability account is credited. When a payment is made to creditors (suppliers) the liability is debited. Thus the normal balance in a liability account is a credit balance. In the example shown below the Accounts payable account has been debited by $1,200 for credit purchases and debited by $500 for payments resulting in a credit balance of $700.

5 of 22
Account Balances - Owner's Equity Accounts for Sole-proprietorships
Owners' equity is increased by credits. The Owner's Capital account is credited to record direct investments in sole-proprietorships. Thus the normal balance in the Capital account is a credit balance.

When a sole proprietor withdraws money, the Drawings account is debited since withdrawals reduce owner's equity. Hence the normal balance in the Drawings account is a debit balance.

6 of 22

Account Balances - Owner's Equity Accounts for Corporations

Owners' equity is increased by credits. Corporations record direct owner investments using the Capital Stock account. Since direct owner investments increase owners' equity, the Capital Stock account is credited. Thus Capital Stock will have a credit balance. Distributions to owners are recorded in the Dividends account. When dividends are declared owners' equity in the business decreases and the Dividends account is debited. Normally, the Retained Earnings account will have a credit balance. However, if a business has had losses, the Retained Earnings account can have a debit balance.

7 of 22

Account Balances - Revenue and Expense Accounts

Owners' equity is increased by credits. When a business earns revenue, usually its total assets increase (Cash or Accounts Receivable or both). This is balanced by an increase in owners' equity. A revenue account is credited to show this increase in owners' equity. Thus revenue accounts will typically have a credit balance.

When a business incurs an expense, owners' equity decreases. An expense account is debited to record this decrease in owners' equity. Thus expense accounts will typically have a debit balance.

8 of 22

Trial balance

After all the transactions have been posted, a trial balance is prepared. As shown on this screen, a trial balance lists each account in the general ledger and its balance (debit or credit) at a particular date. The total of the amounts in the debits column must equal the total credits. If the two amounts do not match there must be an error in the recording. For example, if only the debit part of an entry is posted then the two amounts will not match.

9 of 22

Income statement

This screen shows the income statement for Music Stop for the month of April, 1998. An income statement shows the profitability of a business over a period of time. It shows the revenue and expense account balances. The difference between revenues earned during a period and the expenses for the period represents the net income for the period. The heading of the statement shows the name of the organization, the title of the statement and the period for which the statement is being prepared.

10 of 22

Retained Earnings and Net Income

The income statement showed the changes to owners' equity resulting from profitable operations of the business. Retained earnings represents the portion of owners' equity created by earning net income and reinvesting the profits in the business. The net income minus any dividends declared represent the reinvested profits. The reinvested profits are added to the beginning retained earnings balance. This gives the following relationship:

Ending Retained Earnings = Beginning Retained Earnings + Net Income - Dividends

11 of 22

Retained Earnings

Note that the Retained Earnings balance on the trial balance ($0) corresponds to the balance in the Retained Earnings account at the beginning of the period. This is because revenues, expenses and dividends are recorded in separate accounts during the fiscal period. Thus the amount of reinvested profits are not accumulated in the Retained Earnings account during the period.

12 of 22

Statement of Retained Earnings

This screen shows the statement of retained earnings for Music Stop for the month of April, 1998. The net income minus any dividends declared represent the reinvested profits. The reinvested profits are added to the beginning retained earnings balance to get the ending retained earnings balance. The heading of the statement shows the name of the organization, the title of the statement and the period for which the statement is being prepared.

13 of 22

Balance Sheet

A balance sheet presents the financial position of an organization on a particular date. It shows the assets, liabilities and owners' equity balances for a company at the end of a fiscal period. Note that the Retained Earnings balance is the ending balance shown in the statement of retained earnings. The heading of the statement shows the name of the organization, the title of the statement and the date at which the statement is being prepared.

18 of 22

Statement of Changes in Owners' Equity

The statement of changes in owners' equity shows transactions affecting owners' equity during a period. Three types of transactions affected owner's equity for Clean-Rite Service: (1) the original investment of $500, (2) the revenues and expenses resulting in a net income of $370 and (3) the withdrawal of $100 by the owner. The heading of the statement shows the name of the organization, the title of the statement and the period for which the statement is being prepared.

19 of 22

Balance Sheet

Balance sheet presents the financial position of an organization on a particular date. It shows the assets, liabilities and owners' equity balances for a company at the end of a fiscal period. Note that balance in the Owner's Capital account is the ending balance shown in the statement of changes in owner's equity. The heading of the statement shows the name of the organization, the title of the statement and the date at which the statement is being prepared.

22 of 22

Summary

The ending balance in an account is the difference between the account's total debits and total credits. Normal Balance refers to whether an account usually has a debit or a credit balance.

A trial balance lists each account in the general ledger and its balance (debit or credit) at a particular date. The total of the amounts in the debits column must equal the total in the credits column.

An income statement reports the revenue and expense account balances. The difference between revenues and expenses represents the net income for the period.

The statement of retained earnings summarizes changes to retained earnings resulting from the business operations of a particular period.

A balance sheet reports the assets, liabilities and owners' equity balances for a business at the end of a fiscal period.

II. Revenue and Expense Recognition

Tutorial - Selected Screens

1 of 19
Learning Objectives
After completing this tutorial you should be able to

Explain the implications of the going concern principle and periodic measurement for accounting information.
Distinguish between accrual and cash basis accounting.
Explain whether a given transaction involves the recognition of revenues or expenses under accrual basis accounting.

2 of 19
Going Concern and Periodicity
Business entities are assumed to be going concerns. This means that unless there is evidence to the contrary, organizations are expected to have an indefinite life.

The periodicity concept refers to the fact that an organization's life is divided into periods such as months, quarters or years in order to report financial information in a timely manner. Businesses report information periodically so that users of financial statements such as investors and creditors can make sound decisions.

3 of 19
Cash Basis and Accrual Basis
In cash basis accounting, revenues and expenses are recognized when the associated cash flow occurs. Assume that a company ships goods on Jan 26, 1995. The customer pays the company on Feb 6. Under cash basis accounting revenue would be recorded on Feb 6.

The accrual basis recognizes revenues when they are earned as part of an organization's operating activities. Expenses are recognized when resources are consumed as part of operating activities. Therefore, in the above example, revenue would be recognized on January 26.

4 of 19
Accrual Accounting and Periodicity
The periodicity concept refers to the fact that an organization's life is divided into periods in order to report financial information in a timely manner. Accrual accounting specifies how revenues and expenses are allocated to the appropriate time periods. Revenues are recognized when earned

regardless of when cash is collected. Similarly, expenses are recognized when incurred, regardless of when the cash is paid.

5 of 19

Accrual Accounting and Going Concern

These revenue and expense recognition rules are also based on the going concern assumption. For example, the company may make a sale in the current period but collect the cash in a subsequent period. Since the sale was made in the current period, revenue is recognized in this period. Further, since we assume the organization is a going concern, we expect that cash will be collected in the future. Hence we record an accounts receivable.

6 of 19

Revenue Recognition

In most cases revenue is recognized when goods are sold or services are rendered. Suppose a company sells goods to customers on credit for $1,000 on June 10, 1997. Revenue is recognized because the goods were sold even though cash has not been collected.

7 of 19

The Matching Principle

The matching principle states that the expenses incurred in one period should be offset against the revenues earned during that period. As explained later, this matching is achieved by relating an expense to a particular product sold. If an expense cannot be matched to a particular product, it may be assigned to the accounting period in which the expense is incurred.

8 of 19

Product and Period Costs

Product costs are costs directly associated with specific goods. These costs are expensed in the period in which the goods are sold. For example, the cost of goods sold is recognized in the period in which the goods are sold.

Period costs are not directly associated with specific goods. These expenses are recognized in the period benefiting from the cost. For example, salaries expense is recognized in the period in which the services were provided.

11 of 19

Cost of Goods Sold

Cost of goods sold is the cost of merchandise sold to customers. Accrual accounting matches the cost of the goods to the revenues produced by selling them. Hence when the goods are purchased an asset (Inventory) is increased. The cost of these goods is recognized as expense only when the goods are sold.

Suppose a company purchases goods for $1,000 in June 1995. It sells these for $1,500 in July 1995. Then the cost of the goods ($1,000) is recognized as an expense in July.

12 of 19

Depreciation

When a fixed asset is purchased, it is recorded as an asset. It is misleading to report the entire cost of the equipment as an expense in the period in which they are purchased since the use of equipment will benefit more than one period. Therefore, accrual accounting records the resource as an asset when it is purchased. The cost of the asset is allocated to expense over the life of the asset. Note that cash may or may not have been paid at purchase. The depreciation expense does not involve the amount of cash that has been paid.

13 of 19

Depreciation

Suppose a company buys a computer for $2,000 on Jan 1, 1997. The computer has a useful life of 4 years. The computer is recorded as an asset on Jan 1, 1997 and allocated to expense over 4 years. Thus $500 is recorded as depreciation expense at the end of each year.

To record depreciation, the depreciation expense account is debited to reflect the portion of the cost of the asset consumed during the period. Further, the value of the asset must be reduced by the amount recognized as being consumed. Instead of reducing the asset account directly, the Accumulated Depreciation account is credited. This account represents the value of the asset allocated to depreciation from the time the asset was acquired.

14 of 19

Accumulated Depreciation

Accumulated Depreciation is a contra account. A contra account offsets another account. By crediting this account rather than the asset account, the accounting system can maintain the original cost of the equipment as well as the total depreciation on the fixed asset since its purchase. The difference between the asset account and the accumulated depreciation is called book value. In the previous example, a computer was purchased for $2,000 on Jan. 1, 1997 and depreciated by $400 each year for 5 years. At the end of 1997, the balance in the Accumulated Depreciation account is $400 and the book value is $1,600 (2,000-400). At the end of 1998, the the balance in the Accumulated Depreciation account is $800 and the book value is $1,200 (2,000-800).

15 of 19

Interest expense

Interest expense is the cost associated with borrowing money during an accounting period. Accrual basis records an expense for the interest each accounting period regardless of when the interest is paid.

Suppose a company borrows $4,000 at 10% interest for one year on Oct 1, 1995. The interest and principal will be paid on Oct 1, 1996. The company should not recognize the entire interest of $400 as expense for 1996. The company used the creditor's money for three months in 1995. Hence, three months' interest ($100) will be recognized as an expense in 1995.

16 of 19

Salaries Expense

Salaries and wages are recognized as an expense in the period in which the employees provide services, even if cash is paid in a later period. Thus salaries earned by employees in June are recognized as an expense in June even if they are paid in July.

19 of 19

Summary

Most organizations are going concerns and are expected to continue in operation indefinitely.

Going concerns report the results of their operations periodically, even though all results of these activities are not fully known and must be estimated.

The accrual basis of accounting measures revenues when resources are created from sales and expenses when resources are consumed in earning revenues. Accrual accounting attempts to match the expenses to the revenues earned by incurring these expenses.

Product costs are costs directly associated with specific goods and expensed when the goods are sold. Period costs are costs which cannot be directly associated with specific goods. These costs are recorded as expenses in the period in which they occur.

MODULE IV

I. ADJUSTING ENTRIES - ACCRUALS

Tutorial - Selected Screens

1 of 20
Learning Objectives
After completing this tutorial you must be able to:

Explain the meaning of the terms accrued revenues and accrued expenses.
Prepare adjusting journal entries to record accrued interest, accrued salaries and other expenses.
Prepare adjusting entries to record accrued revenues.

2 of 20
Adjusting Entries
Adjusting entries are prepared at the end of a fiscal period. These entries are required for accrual accounting because of timing differences between cash flows and the recognition of revenues or expenses.

For example, the cost of employee services is recognized as expense in the period the services are provided regardless of when cash is paid to employees. Thus salaries earned by employees in April are recorded as expense in April even if the cash is paid in May.

3 of 20
Accrued Expenses
Accrued expenses occur when expenses are recognized before cash is paid.

4 of 20
Accruing Interest
Interest is accrued for the use of borrowed money during a period if the cash payment for interest will be made in a future period. This transaction is an example of an accrued expense since the expense is recognized before the cash is paid.

Interest is calculated using the following formula:
$i = p * t * r / 100$
p is the principal.
r is the annual rate of interest.
t is the time in years for which the interest is being calculated.
i is the interest for this time period.

5 of 20
Example
A company signed a 12%, $10,000 note payable on July 1, 1998. The note and the interest will be paid on June 30, 1999.
Interest on this debt accumulates throughout the fiscal period. Management recognizes this expense during the period in which it is incurred rather than waiting until cash is paid. The interest expense recorded on Dec 31, 1998 is the amount of interest owed to creditors for the use of the

borrowed money for six months (from July 1 to December 31).

6 of 20
Interest Calculation
Interest for July 1 to December 31, 1998

i = p * t * r / 100
= 10000 * 0.5 year * 12 / 100
= $600
The total interest on the note from July 1, 1998 to June 30,1999
(10,000 * 1 * 12/100= $1,200) will be paid on June 30,1999.

7 of 20
Example
This screen shows the recording of the note on July 1, 1998. The next two screens discuss the accrual of interest and the payment of the note respectively. The organization has obtained money. Hence, cash increases. Further, the business owes $10,000. Thus a liability (Notes Payable) must be recorded for this amount.

8 of 20
Example
Interest is accrued for July 1 to December 31 as shown above. The interest for this period is recognized as expense. Further, the interest payment must be made in the future. The amount of interest to be paid later is recorded as a payable. When the cash is paid this payable will be reduced.

9 of 20
Example
The note is repaid on June 30,1999. The amount borrowed was recorded as a liability (Notes Payable). Now this liability is decreased (debited) by $10,000. Cash is credited by the same amount.

10 of 20
Example
The total interest for one year is $1,200. Hence, total cash paid is $11,200. The amount borrowed was recorded as a liability (Notes Payable). Now this liability is decreased (credited) by $10,000. Further, interest for the use of borrowed funds from Jan 1,1999 to June 30,1999 must be recognized as expense for this period. Thus Interest Expense is debited for $600. Finally, Interest Payable was credited for $600 when interest expense for 1998 was accrued. Now this liability is reduced since the cash is paid.

11 of 20
Accrued Salaries
The previous screens discussed accrual of interest expense. This screen shows another example of accrued expenses. Salaries earned by employees in a period to be paid in a later period are called accrued salaries. Assume $1,000 of salaries earned by employees in December 1997 will be paid in January 1998.

12 of 20

Accrued Salaries

The cost of services provided by employees during 1997 must be recorded as expense for 1997, even if the payment is made in a later period. Hence, salaries expense of $1,000 is accrued on Dec 31, 1997. Since salaries of $1,000 must be paid in the future, a liability (Salaries Payable) is recognized for this amount. When the salary is paid, the liability will be reduced.

13 of 20

Other Accrued Expenses

The previous screens discussed accrual of interest expense and salaries expense. This screen shows another example of accrued expenses. Assume that a company advertised during December 1997. The company has not received a bill or paid for the advertisement. The next screen shows the recording of accrued expense for advertising costs incurred in December.

14 of 20

Example-Advertising Expenses

The advertising costs incurred during 1997 must be recorded as expense for 1997, even if the payment is made in a later period. Hence, advertising expense of $450 is accrued on Dec 31, 1997. Since a payment of $450 must be made in the future, a liability (Accounts Payable) is recognized for this amount. When the payment for the advertisement is made, the liability will be reduced.

17 of 20

Accrued Revenues

Accrued revenues occur when revenues are recognized before cash is received.

18 of 20

Accrued Revenues

Assume that an organization provided services for $500 during December, 1997. The organization has not billed the customer or recorded the sale of services. Accrual accounting recognizes revenue when goods are provided. Since services were provided in December, revenue must be recognized in December. Thus an adjusting entry is prepared on Dec 31, 1997.

19 of 20

Accrued Revenues

This screen shows the journal entry for the transaction described on the previous screen. Since services were provided in December, revenue must be recognized in December. The amount of future payments from customers is recorded as an asset (Accounts Receivable).

20 of 20

Summary

Adjusting entries are prepared at the end of a fiscal period. These entries are required for accrual accounting because of timing differences between cash flows and the recognition of revenues or expenses.

Accrued expenses occur when expenses are recognized before cash is paid. For example, cost of services provided by employees which will be paid in a later period is accrued as salaries expense. Interest is accrued for the use of borrowed money during a period if the cash payment for interest will be made in a future period.

Accrued revenues occur when revenues are recognized before cash is received.

II. ADJUSTING ENTRIES - DEFERRALS

Tutorial - Selected Screens

1 of 21
Learning Objectives
After completing this tutorial you must be able to:

Explain the meaning of the terms deferred revenues and deferred expenses.
Prepare adjusting journal entries to record depreciation of fixed assets, use of supplies and prepaid expenses, and the earning of deferred revenues.

2 of 21
Overview
Adjusting entries are prepared at the end of a fiscal period. These entries are required for accrual accounting because of timing differences between cash flows and the recognition of revenues or expenses.

For example, a company may pay rent in advance for three months on June 1. At the time of the cash payment no expense is recognized. Rent expense is recognized later, at the end of each of the periods benefitting by this advance payment. Thus adjusting entries would be required at the end of June, July and August.

3 of 21
Adjusting Entries - Deferrals
Deferred expenses occur when expenses are recognized after cash is paid.

4 of 21
Prepaid Rent
A company pays two months rent ($1,200) in advance on Dec 1, 1997. Prepare the adjusting entry on Dec 31st to record the rent expense.

Cash was paid in advance for renting the building, equipment etc. At the time cash was paid, the organization records an asset (Prepaid Rent). At the end of the period, the cost of renting the resource is recorded as an expense and Prepaid rent is reduced.

5 of 21
Example
Cash ($1,200) is paid in advance for renting a building for two months. The decrease in cash is recorded by crediting Cash. Further, the advance payment is recorded as an asset Prepaid Rent. This is because accrual basis matches the costs incurred to the benefits earned by incurring these costs. Thus the rent for December will be recognized as expense at the end of December.

6 of 21
Example
Cash ($1,200) was paid in advance for renting a building for two months. At the time cash was paid, Prepaid Rent was increased by $1,200. On Dec 31, the cost of renting the resource in December is recorded as an expense. Prepaid rent is reduced by the amount recognized as expense.

7 of 21

Supplies

Suppose a company has $2,500 of supplies on December 1, 1997. The company purchased supplies for $500 during December. At the end of the period $800 of supplies are available.

When an organization purchases supplies, it records them as an asset. As the organization uses the supplies, it must recognize an expense reflecting the amount of supplies consumed during a period.

8 of 21

Example

When supplies were purchased they were recorded as an asset. As they are consumed, the cost of supplies used must be recorded as expense and the asset account must be decreased. The organization may use the supplies continuously during a period. However, it may not be possible to record the use continuously. Instead, the company calculates the amount used during a period based on beginning and ending quantities and purchases during a period.

Supplies used = beginning supplies + purchases - ending supplies

= 2500 + 500 - 800 = 2200

Thus the supplies expense for the period is $2200.

9 of 21

Example

The cost of supplies used was calculated on the previous screen. At the end of the period, the cost of supplies used is recorded as an expense. The asset Supplies is reduced by the same amount.

10 of 21

Depreciation

The concept of depreciation on fixed assets was discussed in module 3. Recall that accrual accounting records resources such as equipment as assets when they are purchased. The cost of the asset is allocated to expense over the life of the asset. Note that cash may or may not have been paid at purchase. The depreciation expense does not involve the amount of cash that has been paid.

11 of 21

Example

Assume that a company purchases equipment for $10,000 on January 1, 1995. The equipment's useful life is 10 years.

An adjusting entry is prepared at the end of each year of the asset's useful life. In this example, depreciation expense of $1,000 is recorded every year. The balance in the Accumulated Depreciation account represents the total amount by which the asset has been depreciated. Thus the balance in the Accumulated Depreciation account at the end of 1996 is $2,000, the balance at end of 1997 is $3,000 .

12 of 21

Book Value

The book value of the asset is the difference between its original cost and the accumulated depreciation. This is the value of the asset reported on the balance sheet. Assuming the cost of the asset is $10,000, and if the depreciation is $1,000 each year, at the end of the first year the book value is $9,000. At the end of the second year the book value is $8,000.

16 of 21

Deferred Revenues

Deferred revenues occur when revenues are recognized after cash is collected from customers.

17 of 21

Example

A firm receives $4,800 in magazine subscriptions in advance for one year on Sept 1, 1997. Record the transaction on Sept 1, 1997 and the adjusting entry on Dec 31, 1997.

18 of 21

Example

On Sept 1, 1997, the company receives $4,800 in cash. However, it has not yet provided the goods or services to the customer. Hence no revenue has been earned. The company owes the customer $4,800 worth of magazines. Hence, a liability (Unearned Revenue) must be recognized. As the goods or services are provided, revenue is recognized and unearned revenue is decreased.

19 of 21

Journal Entry on September 1, 1997

On Sept 1, 1998, the company receives $4,800 in cash. However, it has not yet provided the goods or services to the customer. Thus, no revenue has been earned. The company owes the customer $4,800 worth of magazines. A liability account (Unearned Revenue) is credited for the amount of goods owed to customers.

20 of 21

Journal Entry on December 31, 1997

The organization has provided a part of the goods/services owed to customers. Since four months subscriptions have been provided, the company has earned ($4800/12) x 4=$1600 in revenue. This is recorded by crediting a revenue account. The customers paid cash in advance. At the time of the cash payment, the company recorded the services owed as a liability (Unearned Revenue). Now this liability is reduced. Thus Unearned Revenue must be debited.

21 of 21

Summary

Deferred expenses occur when expenses are recognized after cash is paid. For example, when supplies are purchased they are recorded as an asset. Expense is recognized later when the supplies are consumed.

Long-term resources such as buildings and equipment are recorded as assets when they are purchased. Their cost is systematically allocated to expense in the periods benefiting from their use.

Deferred revenues occur when cash is collected from customers before goods/services are provided. Revenue is recognized later when the goods/services are provided.

III. CLOSING ENTRIES

Tutorial - Selected Screens

1 of 15
Learning Objectives
After completing this tutorial you must be able to:

Prepare closing entries for corporations.
Prepare closing entries for proprietorships and partnerships.

2 of 15
Closing Revenues and Expenses
Revenue and expense accounts are first closed to a temporary account called Income Summary.

Revenue accounts have a credit balance. To reset the revenue account to zero, it must be debited by an amount equal to its current balance. Income Summary is credited by an equal amount.

Expense accounts have a credit balance. To reset expense accounts to zero, each expense account must be credited by an amount equal to it's current balance. Income Summary is debited by an amount equal to the total expenses.

Finally, the Income Summary account is closed to the Capital account.

3 of 15
Closing the Drawings Account
Owners may receive cash payments from the business. Proprietorships and partnerships use Drawings accounts to record withdrawals during a period. At the end of the period the balance in the Drawings account must also be reset to 0. This balance is subtracted from the Proprietor's Capital (Partner's Capital) accounts.

Since the Drawings account has a debit balance, it must be credited by an equal amount during the closing process. The Capital account is debited by the same amount.

9 of 15
Closing Entries for Corporations
The closing process for corporations also resets revenue and expense accounts to 0, and transfers these balances to an owners' equity account. Corporations record reinvested profits in the Retained Earnings account. Hence, the balances in the revenue and expense accounts are transferred to the Retained Earnings account at the end of the period.

Owners may receive cash payments from the business. Corporations use the Dividends account to record distributions to owners during a period. At the end of the period the balance in the Dividends account must also be reset to 0. This balance is subtracted from the Retained Earnings account.

15 of 15
Summary

The closing process is the final step in the accounting cycle. The closing process resets balances in revenue and expense accounts to zero so that net income for the next period can be measured.

First, revenue and expense accounts are closed to a temporary Income Summary account.

For proprietorships (partnerships) the balance in the Income Summary account is closed to the Proprietor's (Partner's) Capital. Finally, the Drawings account is closed to the Owner's Capital account.

For corporations, the balance in the Income Summary account is closed to the Retained Earnings account . Corporations record cash distributions to owners in the Dividends account. The Dividends account is also closed to Retained Earnings.

Module V

Accounts Receivable

Tutorial - Selected Screens

1 of 24
Learning Objectives
After completing this tutorial you should be able to:

Calculate uncollectible accounts expense using the Percentage of Sales method and the Aging Method.
Record uncollectible accounts expense using the Allowance method.
Prepare a journal entry to write-off a customer account under the Allowance method.

2 of 24
Overview
Previous tutorials discussed the recording of credit sales. Recall that when goods or services are sold on credit, Accounts Receivable is debited and Revenue is credited. Selling on credit enables a company to increase revenues and net income since customers unable to pay immediately may make a credit purchase. However, the business may fail to collect from some credit customers. The amounts that cannot be collected are called uncollectible accounts. Uncollectible accounts expense is an expense of selling on credit.

This tutorial extends the discussion of accounts receivable in prior tutorials by explaining how information about uncollectible accounts is recorded in the accounting system.

3 of 24
Recognizing Uncollectible Accounts Expense
As discussed on the previous screen, the amount not collectible from customers is an expense. A key question related to recognizing this expense is: When should uncollectible accounts expense be recognized?

For example, assume that a company makes a credit sale in November 1997. In July 1998, after making several collection efforts, the company decides that the customer's account is uncollectible. One option is to record an expense when a customer's account becomes uncollectible. Thus in this example, the company could record the expense in 1998. Since the revenue from these credit sales was recognized in 1997, this approach does not match the uncollectible accounts expense with the revenue it helped produce.

4 of 24
Allowance Method
An alternative approach is to recognize the uncollectible accounts expense in the same accounting period as the revenues it helped produce. Thus, in the previous example, the uncollectible accounts resulting from sales in 1997 should be

recognized in 1997. This approach is called the allowance method. The allowance method is used by companies with large credit sales because it provides better matching of the uncollectible accounts expense and revenues.

Since the business may not know which accounts are uncollectible until a later period, uncollectible accounts must be estimated and recorded at the end of the accounting period. The next screen describes the recording of bad debts once an estimate has been made. The methods used to estimate bad debts are described later in this tutorial.

5 of 24

Recording Uncollectible Accounts

Under the allowance method, uncollectible accounts are estimated and recorded at the end of every period. The recording of uncollectible accounts has two effects. First, Uncollectible Accounts Expense is debited. This expense is subtracted from revenues on the income statement and reduces net income.

In addition to the expense, uncollectible accounts also effectively decrease accounts receivable. However, instead of directly crediting Accounts Receivable, a contra asset called Allowance for Uncollectible Accounts is credited.

6 of 24

Net Realizable Value of Accounts Receivable

The Accounts Receivable, the Allowance account and the net realizable value of accounts receivable are shown on the balance sheet. The net realizable value is an estimate of the amount management expects to collect on the total accounts receivable.

Net Realizable value of Accounts Receivable	=	Accounts Receivable	-	Allowance for Bad debts

9 of 24

Writing off an uncollectible account

As explained previously, under the Allowance method, an Allowance for Uncollectible Accounts is credited for the amount of estimated uncollectible accounts at the end of every period. The Accounts Receivable balance is reduced only when specific accounts are identified as uncollectible. When a specific customer account is identified as uncollectible, it is written off against the Allowance for Uncollectible Accounts. Thus a specific account is written off by debiting Allowance for Uncollectible Accounts and crediting Accounts Receivable.

13 of 24

Previous screens discussed the recording of Uncollectible Accounts Expense and write-off of specific customer accounts. The remainder of this tutorial describes the methods used to estimate uncollectible accounts.

Two methods are used to estimate uncollectible accounts
Percentage of Sales
Accounts Receivable Aging Method

14 of 24

Percentage of Sales Method

One approach used by businesses to estimate uncollectible accounts is to compute Uncollectible Accounts Expense as a percentage of total credit sales. The idea behind this approach is that Uncollectible Accounts Expense is directly related to the amount of credit sales.

Assume that Sanchez Company had credit sales of $40,000 in 1998. Based on prior experience, Johnson Manufacturing estimates that 3% of its credit sales will be uncollectible.

Uncollectible Accounts Expense = .03 x 40,000 = $1,200

15 of 24

Accounts Receivable Aging method

Recall that the percentage of sales method assumes that some portion of credit sales for the period will become uncollectible. The idea behind the Accounts Receivable Aging method is that some percentage of a company's ending accounts receivable balance will become uncollectible. This approach calculates the required balance in the Allowance for Uncollectible Accounts as a percentage of the ending Accounts Receivable balance. The current balance in the Allowance account is compared to the required balance to determine the amount of Uncollectible Accounts Expense.

16 of 24

Accounts Receivable Aging method

To calculate the required balance in the allowance account, an analysis of the total accounts receivables by age is prepared. The aging analysis shows groups of outstanding accounts receivables by due date. For example, accounts due for less than 30 days could be listed in one column of the aging report. Other columns could list balances due between 31-60 days, 61-90 days etc. Management estimates the probability that balances in each category will not be collected. These estimates are made under the assumption that the longer an amount is outstanding, the more likely it will be uncollectible. The next screen shows an example of the use of the aging method to calculate the required balance in the Allowance account.

18 of 24

Accounts Receivable Aging Method

The previous screen estimated the required balance in the Allowance account to be $585. Assume that the current balance Allowance account is $150. The Allowance account must be credited for $585-150=$435. The journal entry to record the uncollectible accounts is shown on the next screen.

24 of 24

Summary

The allowance method recognizes uncollectible accounts expense in the same accounting period as the revenues it helped produce. Since the business may not know which accounts are uncollectible until a later period, the uncollectible accounts expense is estimated and recorded at the end of the accounting period.

To record uncollectible accounts, Uncollectible Accounts Expense is debited and an Allowance for Uncollectible Accounts is credited.

When a specific customer account is identified as uncollectible, it is written off against the Allowance for Uncollectible Accounts. Thus a specific account is written off by debiting Allowance for Uncollectible Accounts and crediting Accounts Receivable.

Two methods are used to estimate uncollectible accounts expense under the allowance method - the percentage of sales method and the aging method.

MODULE V

Inventory

Tutorial - Selected Screens

1 of 27
Learning Objectives
After completing this tutorial you should be able to:

Calculate cost of goods sold and ending inventory using the LIFO, FIFO and weighted average methods under the periodic inventory system.
Calculate cost of goods sold and ending inventory using the LIFO and FIFO methods under the perpetual inventory system.

2 of 27
Overview
Merchandising firms sell goods to customers. Goods for sale are recorded as an asset (Inventory) when they are purchased. Inventory is reduced when the goods the goods are sold. Also the cost of the goods is recognized as an expense (Cost of Goods Sold) when the goods are sold.

Most firms purchase inventory on an ongoing basis. the prices of the goods may not remain constant throughout an accounting period. At any given time, the cost of the different units in inventory is different. Thus when goods are sold businesses must determine the cost of the specific items sold. This tutorial describes various cost flow assumptions used by businesses when inventory prices vary during a period.

3 of 27
Flow of Inventory Costs
A business typically starts each year with some merchandise left over from the previous period. This inventory is beginning inventory for the period. During the period inventory is purchased. The beginning inventory and the purchases together make up the total goods available for sale. The sum of the costs of the beginning inventory and the purchases is called the cost of goods available for sale.

During the period the business sells some inventory. The remaining inventory is called the ending inventory. The difference between the cost of goods available for sale and the ending inventory is the cost of goods sold. These relationships are illustrated graphically on the next screen.

5 of 27
Periodic Inventory System
Businesses use two types of systems to keep track of information about inventory and for calculating the cost of goods sold and ending inventory - the periodic method and the perpetual method.

Under the periodic system, the business starts a period with information about the beginning inventory, purchases are recorded throughout the period. However, the business does not continuously update the inventory balances. Rather, a physical count of inventory is taken at the end of the period. Cost of goods sold is calculated from information about beginning inventory, ending inventory (obtained by physical count) and purchases.

6 of 27

Perpetual Inventory System

In a perpetual inventory system the business keeps a continuous record of inventory. Information about events affecting inventory (purchases and sales) are immediately recorded in the system . The records show the current inventory balance at all times.

7 of 27

Inventory Costing Methods

This section of the tutorial describes different inventory costing methods used by businesses. The cost of goods sold and the ending inventory can be easily determined if the unit cost of the goods purchased during a period remains constant. However, the unit cost often changes. When the goods are sold, accountants must have some way of determining the unit cost of the items sold. This tutorial describes three approaches used to compute cost of goods sold:

Last in, first out (LIFO)
First in, first out (FIFO)
Weighted-average cost

8 of 27

Inventory Costing Methods

Under LIFO (last in, first out), a business keeps records of all the purchases. The units of inventory purchased last are assumed to be sold first. For example, assume that a business has 10 units in beginning inventory with unit cost $1.20 and purchases 20 units at $1.50. Assume that 8 items are sold. Under LIFO, the 8 items sold are assumed to be from the units purchased. Thus cost of goods sold under LIFO is 8x1.5=$12.

FIFO assumes that the goods purchased first are sold first. If FIFO were used in the previous example, the 8 items sold would be assumed to be from the beginning inventory. Thus cost of goods sold under FIFO is 8x1.2 = $9.6. Note that when prices are rising, cost of goods sold is lower under FIFO.

9 of 27

Inventory Costing Methods

The weighted-average cost method is based on the weighted average of the inventory during the period.

Average cost = Cost of goods Available for Sale/ units available for sale

Recall that cost of goods available for sale equals the beginning inventory plus purchases.

In the previous example,

average cost/unit = (10x1.2+20x1.5)/30
= $1.4
Cost of goods sold = 8x1.4 = $11.2

18 of 27

Inventory Costing Methods - Perpetual System

Recall that the FIFO method assumes that the goods purchased first are sold first. Under LIFO (last in, first out) the units of inventory purchased last are assumed to be sold first. These cost flow assumptions are also used in perpetual inventory systems.

However, the two cost flow assumptions are applied differently in perpetual systems as explained below: Under the periodic system, the cost of goods sold is only calculated at the end of the period. Thus the last(first) units refer to the last(first) units purchased n the period. Under the perpetual system cost of goods sold is calculate as sales are made. The last(first) units refer to the last(first) units purchased at the time of the sale (not the end of the period).

19 of 27

Inventory Costing Methods - Perpetual System

Under the periodic system, the cost of goods sold is only calculated at the end of the period. Under the perpetual system cost of goods sold is calculate as sales are made. Thus the last goods in inventory at the time of the sale are considered to be sold first. For example, assume that a business had 5 units of an item in beginning inventory, purchased 10 units in March and 12 units in August. Assume that 3 units were sold in May. Then at the time of the sale the last units in inventory are from the purchase in March. Thus the 3 units sold are assumed to be from the purchase in March.

27 of 27

Summary

Under the periodic system, a business keeps records of the beginning inventory and purchases continuously. A physical count is taken at the end of the period to compute the ending inventory and the cost of goods sold.

Under the perpetual method, a business tracks purchases and sales continuously. The cost of the goods sold is computed at the time of the sale.

Different cost flow assumptions are used in periodic and perpetual inventory systems. The FIFO cost flow method assumes that the goods purchased first are sold first. The LIFO method (last in, first out) assumes that the units of inventory purchased last are assumed to be sold first. The weighted-average cost method computes the weighted-average cost of the goods available for sale. This unit cost is used to compute cost of goods sold and ending inventory.

MODULE V

Plant Assets

Tutorial - Selected Screens

1 of 17
Learning Objectives
After completing this tutorial you should be able to:

Calculate depreciation expense using the straight-line method.
Calculate depreciation expense using the double-declining balance method.
Record the sale of an asset for gain or loss.

2 of 17
Overview
Recall from previous tutorials that when a fixed asset is purchased, it is recorded as an asset. The cost of the asset allocated to expense in every period is called depreciation expense.

To record depreciation, the depreciation expense account is debited. Further, the Accumulated Depreciation account is credited to reduce the value of the asset by the amount recognized as being consumed. The Accumulated Depreciation account represents the value of the asset allocated to depreciation from the time the asset was acquired.

This tutorial describes two methods used by organizations to calculate depreciation - the straight-line method and the double-declining balance method.

3 of 17
Review of key terms
The following are required to calculate depreciation:

Cost : Cost is the price at which the asset was purchased.

Useful life: The estimated useful life is the length of service the business expects from an asset. For example, the useful life of a computer is the number of years the computer is expected to be used.

Salvage Value: The expected cash value of the asset at the end of it's useful life is called salvage value.

Depreciable cost: The cost of the asset minus the salvage value is called depreciable cost.

4 of 17

Straight-line Method

The straight-line method allocates an equal amount of depreciation expense to each period of the asset's useful life. Depreciation Expense is calculated using the formula:

Depreciation = Depreciable cost/useful life
Expense = (Cost - Salvage value)/ Useful life

At the end of each period the depreciation for that period is added to the accumulated depreciation. Thus accumulated depreciation is the total depreciation from the date the asset was purchased to the current date. The difference between the cost and accumulated depreciation is called the book value of the asset.

7 of 17

Double-declining Balance Method

The double-declining balance method is an accelerated method. Accelerated methods for calculating depreciation allocate larger amounts to depreciation expense in the earlier periods of the useful life than in later periods.

In this method, depreciation expense is calculated as follows:

First, the straight-line depreciation rate is calculated.
Straight-line depreciation rate = 1/useful life

Then the double-declining balance rate is calculated.
Double-declining balance rate = 2 x Straight-line rate

8 of 17

Double-declining Balance Method

Depreciation expense is computed by multiplying the double-declining-balance(DDB) rate by the book value of the asset at the beginning of the period. For the first period, the book value is equal to the cost of the asset. For each subsequent period, book value is the difference between the cost of the asset and the accumulated depreciation. Thus

Depreciation expense = Book value x DDB rate

Note that the asset must not be depreciated below the salvage value. If the amount of depreciation expense for a year calculated using the above formula will reduce the book value below salvage, then the amount of depreciation expense is the amount needed to reduce the asset's book value to the salvage value.

13 of 17

Disposal of plant assets

Businesses dispose of plant assets after they cease to meet their needs. Businesses may dispose of plant assets by selling or exchanging it. If the asset cannot be sold or exchanged, the asset may be discarded. This tutorial discusses the sale of assets only.

When an asset is sold, the business recognizes a gain or loss. If the price at which the asset is sold is greater than it's book value at the time of the sale then a gain is recognized. If the price at which the asset is sold is less than it's book value then a loss is recognized.

14 of 17

Disposal of plant assets

Suppose a business sells furniture on January 1, 2001 for $6,000. The furniture was purchased on January 1, 1998 for $10,000. Its useful life is 10 years and salvage value is 0. Assume that the business uses the straight-line method for calculating depreciation.

At the time of the sale, the business has used the asset for 3 years (1998,1999, 2000). In each of these years, depreciation expense of $1,000 ($10,000/10) is recognized. Thus Accumulated Depreciation is $3,000 at the time of the sale. The book value of the asset is $10.000-3,000=$7,000 at the time of the sale. The price at which the asset is sold ($,6000) is less than the book value of $7,000. Thus a loss of $1,000 is recognized. The next screen shows the journal entry for the sale.

17 of 17

Summary

This tutorial described two methods for calculating depreciation - 1) the straight-line method and 2) the double-declining balance method. The straight-line method allocates an equal amount of depreciation expense to each period of the asset's useful life.

The double-declining balance method is an accelerated method. Accelerated methods for calculating depreciation allocate larger amounts to depreciation expense in the earlier periods of the useful life than in later periods.

When an asset is sold. the business recognizes a gain or loss. If the price at which the asset is sold is greater than it's book value at the time of the sale then a gain is recognized. If the price at which the asset is sold is less than it's book value then a loss is recognized.

MODULE VI

Liabilities and Owners' Equity

I. Bonds

Tutorial - Selected Screens

1 of 22
Learning Objectives
After completing this tutorial you should be able to:

Record the issuance of bonds at par, at a discount and at a premium.
Calculate interest payments and amortization of discount or premium using the straight-line method.
Record the periodic payment or accrual of interest on the bonds.

2 of 22
Overview
Accompany needing a large amount of money maybe unable to get it from one creditor. Bonds are a form of debt where money is borrowed from multiple lenders. Bonds Payable are contracts between an organization and the lenders in which the borrower agrees to repay the amount borrowed at specified dates and to pay specified amounts of interest.

Most corporate bonds are paid at the end of debt's life. The final amount to be paid to the bondholders is called the face value of the bond. The specified date at which this amount is to be paid is called the maturity date. The annual interest paid on the bond is called the stated rate of interest. As an example, assume that Cottell Corporation issues $100,000 of 8%, five-year bonds on January 1, 1998. In this case the face value of $100,000 is paid on January 1, 2003 (maturity date). Interest paid every year is $8,000 (.08 x $100,000).

3 of 22
Stated and Market Rates
As explained on the previous screen, an annual rate of interest is specified for bonds. This interest rate is called the stated rate. The amount of interest paid by the issuer of the bond equals the face value of the bond multiplied by the stated rate. The market rate is the rate that creditors demand for loaning their money. The rate that creditors are willing to accept depends on the level of risk associated with the investment.

Bond issuers may decide on a stated rate of interest equal to the rate they expect the market to demand at the time of issue. However, the actual market rate at the time of issue may not be equal to the stated rate. If the two rates are equal the bonds are issued at face value, otherwise the issue price is different from the face value.

5 of 22
Issuing Bonds at a Discount or Premium
If the market rate is higher than the stated rate, then the bonds are issued at a discount.

In the previous example, if the market rate is 10% and the stated rate is 8%, investors are not willing to pay the face value because they can get a better rate on other investments of similar risk. The amount by which the face value exceeds the price at which the bonds are sold is called the discount on bonds payable.

If the market rate is lower than the stated rate, then the bonds are issued at a premium. In the previous example, if the market rate was 7.5% and the stated rate is 8%, investors are willing to pay more than the face value because the bonds pay more than other investments of similar risk. The amount by which the issue price of the bonds exceeds the face value is called the premium on bonds payable.

8 of 22

Interest Expense on Bonds Issued at a Discount

Assume that a company issues 8-year, 10% bonds for $100,000 at 95. Interest is paid semi-annually on Jan. 1 and Jul. 1. The company pays $10,00 (0.1 x $100,000) interest annually. Each semi-annual interest payment is $5,000 ($10,000 x1/2). The issue price of the bonds is $95,000 (.95 x $100,000). However, the company pays $100,000 to the bondholders at the end of the eight years. The difference of $5,000 between the face value and the issue price (discount) is also a cost of borrowing money (interest). Thus the total interest cost incurred by the company on the bonds includes the semi-annual interest payments of $5,000 as well as the discount of $5,000.

The next screen describes how the total interest expense is calculated for each period.

9 of 22

Amortization of Bond Discount

As explained on the previous screen, the discount of $5,000 is also part of the overall interest on the bonds. Accrual accounting matches expenses to the revenues earned by incurring those expenses. Rather than allocate the entire discount of $5,000 to interest expense at the time of issue of the bonds, this difference is temporarily assigned to a Discount on Bonds Payable account. The discount is then systematically allocated to expense. The process of assigning the discount to interest expense is called amortization.

The difference between the face value of the bond and the discount is called the carrying value of the bond. As the discount is amortized over the life of the bond, the amount of discount decreases. Correspondingly, the carrying value of the bond increases over the life of the bond. The carrying value equals face value on the maturity date. This tutorial describes one method of amortization - the straight-line method.

10 of 22

Discount Amortization - Straight-line Method

In the previous example, a company issues 8-year, 10% bonds for $100,000 at 95. Interest is paid semi-annually on Jan. 1 and Jul. 1. The straight-line method allocates equal amounts to discount over each period of the bond's life. In this example, the discount of $5,000 is allocated to interest expense over 8 years. The amount allocated per year equals $625 ($5,000/2). Since interest is paid semi-annually,

$312.5 ($625 x 1/2) of the discount is allocated to interest expense every six months.

Also, the company pays $10,000 (0.1 x $100,000) interest annually. Each semi-annual interest payment is $5,000 ($10,000 x1/2). Thus total interest expense recorded semi-annually is $5,312.5 ($5,000 + $312.5).

16 of 22

Interest Expense on Bonds Issued at a Premium

Assume that Schon Company issues 4-year, 10% bonds for $100,000 at 102. Interest is paid semi-annually on Jan. 1 and Jul. 1. The company pays $10,000 (0.1 x $100,000)interest annually. Each semi-annual interest payment is $5,000 ($10,000 x1/2). The issue price of the bonds is $102,000 (1.02 x $100,000). However, the company pays $100,000 to the bondholders at the end of the eight years. Since the amount paid at maturity is $2,000 lower than the amount obtained from creditors at the time of issue, this difference of $2,000 can be viewed as reduction in the cost of borrowing money (interest). Thus the total interest cost incurred by the company on the bonds equals the total of the semi-annual interest payments of $5,000 minus the premium of $2,000.

The next screen describes how the total interest expense is calculated for each period.

17 of 22

Amortization of Bond Premium

As explained on the previous screen, the premium of $2,000 must be subtracted from the total of the semi-annual interest payments to calculate the overall interest on the bonds. Accrual accounting matches expenses to the revenues earned by incurring those expenses. Rather than allocate the entire premium of $2,000 to interest expense at the time of issue of the bonds, this difference is temporarily assigned to a Premium on Bonds Payable account. The premium is then systematically allocated to expense. The process of assigning the premium to interest expense is called amortization.

The sum of the face value of the bond and the premium is called the carrying value of the bond. As the premium is amortized over the life of the bond, the amount of premium decreases. Correspondingly, the carrying value of the bond decreases over the life of the bond. The carrying value equals face value on the maturity date.

18 of 22

Premium Amortization - Straight-line Method

In the previous example, a company issues 4-year, 10% bonds for $100,000 at 102. Interest is paid semi-annually on Jan. 1 and Jul. 1. The straight-line method allocates equal amounts to premium over each period of the bond's life. In this example, the premium of $2,000 is allocated to interest expense over 4 years. The amount allocated per year equals $500 ($2,000/4). Since interest is paid semi-annually, $250 ($500 x 1/2) of the premium is allocated to interest expense every six months.

Also, the company pays $10,000 (0.1 x $100,000)interest annually. Each semi-annual interest payment is $5,000 ($10,000 x1/2). Thus total interest expense recorded semi-annually is $4,750 ($5,000 - $250).

Summary

Bonds Payable are contracts between an organization and the lenders in which the borrower agrees to repay the amount borrowed at specified dates and to pay specified amounts of interest. Most corporate bonds are paid at the end of debt's life. The final amount to be paid to the bondholders is called the face value of the bond.

Bonds are issued at par when the stated rate of interest equals the market rate of interest. When the stated rate is lower than the market rate, bonds are issued at a discount. The discount is amortized over the life of the bond. The interest expense for each period equals the interest paid to bondholders plus the discount amortization. When the stated rate is higher than the market rate, bonds are issued at a premium. The premium is amortized over the life of the bond. The interest expense for each period equals the interest paid to bondholders minus the premium amortization.

II. Corporate Transactions

Tutorial - Selected Screens

1 of 21
Learning Objectives
After completing this tutorial you should be able to:

Record the issuance of common and preferred stock.
Record the declaration and payment of dividends.
Record the purchase of treasury stock.
Understand stock dividends and stock splits.

2 of 21
Overview
A corporation is recognized under the law as a distinct entity from the owners. The owners of the corporation are not personally liable for the debts of the business. The owners of the corporation have limited liability since they cannot lose any more than the amounts invested in the business.

Ownership of the corporation is divided into shares of capital stock and the owners are called stockholders. Owners can sell all or part of their shares to other investors. Managers of a corporation manage the day-to-day operations of the business. Managers may or may not be stockholders. Thus there is a separation of ownership and management of corporations.

3 of 21
Common Stock
Corporations often issue more than one type of stock. The most basic type is called common stock. Each share of common stock represents an equal share in the ownership of the corporation. Shares of common stock are often issued with a par value. The par value is an arbitrary value assigned to a share of stock. Many states require par value to specified in the charter.

Stock is usually sold at a price greater than par value. The amount received by a corporation in excess of the par value is called Contributed Capital in Excess of Par. Assume that Brown Corporation issues 5000 shares of $5 par value stock for $7 per share. The total cash received is $35,000 (5,000 x $7). The par value of the stock issued is $25,000 (5,000 x $5). The Contributed Capital in Excess of Par is $10,000 ($35,000 - $25,000).

4 of 21
Issuance of Common Stock
This screen shows how the issuance of 5000 shares of stock of par value $5 by Brown Corporation for $7 per share is recorded in the journal. Cash is debited by $35,000 (5,000 x $7). The account Common Stock is credited by the par value of the stock issued $25,000 (5,000 x $5). The Contributed Capital in Excess of Par is credited by $10,000 ($35,000 - $25,000).

5 of 21

Treasury Stock

Stock repurchased by a company from its shareholders is called treasury stock. A company may buy its own stock for providing to employees as compensation, to avoid hostile takeover by investors or to maintain the market for the shares. The journal entry for purchase of $2,000 shares of stock of par value 10 from investors at $11 each is given below. Cash is credited by $22,000 (2,000 x $11). The account Treasury Stock is debited by the same amount. Treasury Stock is a contra equity account since it reduces the total owners' equity.

6 of 21

Authorized, Issued and Outstanding Shares

Corporations must be chartered by a state. The charter specifies several things such as the par value of the stock and the number of shares a corporation is authorized to issue. A corporation may not issue all the shares it is authorized to issue. Issued shares are shares that have been sold to investors.

Outstanding shares are shares currently held by investors. When a company purchases treasury stock, the number of outstanding shares decreases. For example, assume that a company which is authorized to issue 50,000 shares sells 40,000 shares to investors. Then the number of shares issued and outstanding is 40,000. Now if the corporation purchases 2,500 shares of its own stock. The number of outstanding shares after the purchase of treasury stock is 37,500 (40,000 -2,500).

7 of 21

Issuing Cash Dividends

Dividends are issued only on outstanding shares. Three dates are important in recording dividend payments. The date of declaration is the date on which the directors announce that the dividend will be paid. A journal entry is prepared and a liability is recognized for the amount of dividend that will be paid.

The date of record is used to identify the investors who will receive the dividends. All shareholders on that date are issued the dividend. No journal entry is required on this date.

The date of payment is the date on which the dividend is paid to investors. A journal entry is prepared to record the dividend payment. The liability recorded on the date of declaration is reduced. The next two screens show the journal entries.

12 of 21

Preferred Stock

Some corporations issue more than one class of stock. Preferred stock is stock with a higher claim to dividends and assets than common stock. Dividends must be paid to preferred stockholders before they can be paid to common stockholders. Preferred stockholders share in the profits of a corporation but usually do not have voting rights.

Preferred stockholders also have preference over common stockholders if a company has to liquidate its assets. Thus preferred stock is less risky than common stock.

However, creditors have a higher preference than preferred stockholders. Thus preferred stock is more risky than debt investments.

13 of 21

Dividends on Preferred Stock

The dividends on preferred stock are usually specified as a percentage of the par value. Assume that Brown Corporation issued 5000 shares of 6%, $50 par value preferred stock on January 1, 1998. The par value of the issued shares is $250,000 (5000 x $50). Then the dividends paid to preferred stockholders each year equals $15,000(0.06 x $250,000).

Assume that Brown Corporation declares dividends of $20,000 in 1998. Then $15,000 would be paid to preferred stockholders. The remaining $5,000 will be paid to common stockholders.

14 of 21

Cumulative Preferred Stock

Preferred stock is often cumulative. If dividends are cumulative and if they are not paid in prior years then dividends for these years must be paid to preferred stockholders before any dividends can be paid to common stockholders. In the previous example, Brown Corporation issued 5000 shares of 6%, $50 par value cumulative preferred stock on January 1, 1998. Assume that dividends paid in 1998 equals $12,000 and that dividends of $27,000 were declared in 1999.

Recall that dividends to be paid to preferred stockholders each year equals $15,000. Since the preferred stockholders only received dividends of $12,000 in 1998, the difference of $3,000 (15,000 -12,000) must be paid in later years. Thus in 1999 preferred stockholders must be paid $18,000 ($15,000 for 1999 and $ 3,000 for 1998) before common stockholders can be paid any dividends. Dividends paid to common stockholders in 1999 equals $9,000

15 of 21

Issuance of Preferred Stock

This screen shows how the issuance of 5000 shares of preferred stock of par value $50 by Brown Corporation for $52 per share is recorded in the journal. Cash is debited by $260,000 (5,000 x $52). The account Common Stock is credited by the par value of the stock issued $250,000 (5,000 x $50). The Contributed Capital in Excess of Par is $10,000 ($260,000 - $250,000).

18 of 21

Stock Dividends

Corporations sometimes issue stock dividends instead of paying cash dividends. Stock dividends are additional shares of stock issued to shareholders without charge. For example, if a corporation with 20,000 outstanding shares issues a 2% stock dividend, the investors are issued 400 (0.02 x 20,000) new shares.

Stock dividends do not involve the payment of cash. It involves the transfer of the amount of the stock dividends from retained earnings to contributed capital. Thus the total stockholders' equity is also not affected.

19 of 21

Stock Dividends

Since stock dividends do not affect cash or equity, the question is: Why do corporations issue stock dividends? Corporations may issue stock dividends instead of cash dividends because they want to use the cash for expansion. Another reason for issuing stock dividends is to keep the price of the stock affordable. As a profitable corporation grows, the price of its stock may increase in anticipation of continued growth and dividend payments. Stock dividends may be issued to increase the number of shares and hence decrease the price per share to keep it attractive for smaller investors

20 of 21

Stock Split

As mentioned previously, one reason for issuing stock dividends is to keep the price of the stock affordable. The same result can also be achieved through a stock split. When a company declared a stock split, the number of outstanding shares are multiplied by some number. For example, if a 2 for 1 split is declared, two shares are issued for every share of the existing stock. The par value of the stock is reduced in the same proportion. For example, if the company issues stock of par value $10 and a 2 for 1 split is declared, the par value after the split is $5.

21 of 21

Summary

This tutorial discussed the recording of several corporate transactions includng the issuance of stock, declaration and payment of dividends and the purchase of treasury stock. The tutorial also discussed preferred stock, stock dividends and stock splits. Preferred stock is stock with a higher claim to dividends and assets than common stock. Dividends must be paid to preferred stockholders before they can be paid to common stockholders. Stock repurchased by a company from its shareholders is called treasury stock. Stock dividends are additional shares of stock issued to shareholders without charge. When a company declares a stock split, the number of outstanding shares are multiplied by some number. The par value of the stock is reduced in the same proportion.

Appendix I
Module 5

Practice Problem 1
Edusoft, Inc.

<u>T-accounts for 1998</u>

Cash

Sales Revenue

Accounts Receivable

Uncollectible Accounts Expense

Allowance for Uncollectible Accounts

Practice Problem 1
Edusoft, Inc.

T-accounts for 1999

Cash

Sales Revenue

Accounts Receivable

Uncollectible Accounts Expense

Allowance for Uncollectible Accounts

Practice Problem 2
Safeco Security Systems

<u>T-accounts for 1998</u>

Cash

Sales Revenue

Accounts Receivable

Uncollectible Accounts Expense

Allowance for Uncollectible Accounts

Practice Problem 2
Safeco Security Systems

T-accounts for 1999

Cash

Sales Revenue

Accounts Receivable

Uncollectible Accounts Expense

Allowance for Uncollectible Accounts

Homework Problem 1
Alden Industries

T-accounts for 1998

Cash

Sales Revenue

Accounts Receivable

Uncollectible Accounts Expense

Allowance for Uncollectible Accounts

Homework Problem 1
Alden Industries

T-accounts for 1999

Cash

Sales Revenue

Accounts Receivable

Uncollectible Accounts Expense

Allowance for Uncollectible Accounts

Homework Problem 2
Schmidt Office Supplies

T-accounts for 1998

Cash

Sales Revenue

Accounts Receivable

Uncollectible Accounts Expense

Allowance for Uncollectible Accounts

Homework Problem 2
Schmidt Office Supplies

<u>T-accounts for 1999</u>

Cash

Accounts Receivable

Allowance for Uncollectible Accounts

Sales Revenue

Uncollectible Accounts Expense

Homework Problem 3
Bedford Windows

T-accounts for 1998

Cash

Sales Revenue

Accounts Receivable

Uncollectible Accounts Expense

Allowance for Uncollectible Accounts

Homework Problem 3
Bedford Windows

T-accounts for 1999

Cash

Sales Revenue

Accounts Receivable

Uncollectible Accounts Expense

Allowance for Uncollectible Accounts

Homework Problem 4
McCoy Company

T-accounts for 1998

Cash

Sales Revenue

Accounts Receivable

Uncollectible Accounts Expense

Allowance for Uncollectible Accounts

Homework Problem 4
McCoy Company

T-accounts for 1999

Cash

Sales Revenue

Accounts Receivable

Uncollectible Accounts Expense

Allowance for Uncollectible Accounts